IN AN

GODS AND TEMPLES

CONTENTS

Beliefs	2
The Gods	6
Temples	16
Priests	24
Worship	26
Festivals	28
Gallery of Gods	30
Glossary and Index	31

SALIMA IKRAM

Illustrations by Riham El Sherbini

HOOPOE BOOKS

Beliefs

It is not easy for us who live in a different time, with our own religions, to understand how the ancient Egyptians thought about their gods and how they practised their beliefs. Although most of what remains from ancient Egypt, such as tombs and temples, is religious, very few writings have survived to explain *why* the Egyptians believed what they did.

The lack of written documents is not the only problem for Egyptologists today. Ancient Egyptian history covers thousands of years and the beliefs of the people changed a lot in that time. It is difficult now to follow all the changes.

Often the ancient Egyptians had two or three different explanations for something, such as how the world was created. Sometimes a story says that the world was created from an ocean, sometimes from an egg, and sometimes from the speaking of magic words. These different stories were all believed at the same time.

The way that ordinary people practised their religion was also different from the official religion with its large temples.

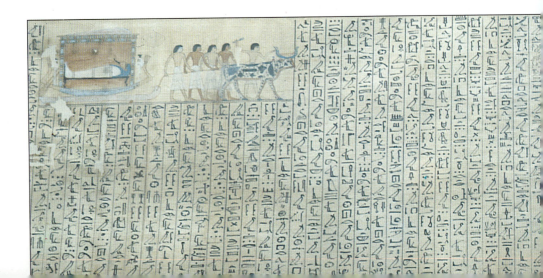

Above: The temple of Horus at Edfu. This is the most complete temple still standing in Egypt.
Below: A chapter from the Book of the Dead, with pictures showing the coffin being taken to the tomb of the dead person, and the person changing into different birds in order to reach the afterlife.

Egyptian religion was based on nature. Much of it tried to explain natural events such as the rising and setting of the sun and the flooding of the river Nile. The gods and goddesses – and many of the stories about them – all come from nature. Many of the deities took the form of animals, or were sometimes shown as part animal, part human.

Natural elements were thought of as male or female, and the gods who represented them were shown as men or women or as a mixture of animals and people. However, one of the greatest natural elements – the river Nile – was not represented by any god.

Above: Although the Nile itself had no god, the annual flood was associated with the god Hapi who was supposed to live in Aswan, in Upper Egypt.

All the gods were worshipped throughout the country. Each also had its own town or towns that were sacred mainly to them. The temple was the centre of all life in the town.

The Egyptians thought of the moon-god, Khonsu, as a young man. The earth-god, Geb, was shown as a man too, but the sky-goddess, Nut, was a woman. This is very unusual because in other ancient religions – such as Greek, Roman and Mesopotamian – the sky was thought of as a male god while the earth and moon were considered to be female.

The sky-goddess Nut stands in an arch over the earth-god Geb.

A large part of ancient Egyptian religion focused on the belief of life after death: the afterlife. The Egyptians believed that the soul of a dead person could live forever. This is why they made beautiful tombs and filled them with things that the dead person could use in the afterlife.

THE GODS

The sun-god Re travelling across the sky in his boat. Re's trip across the sky by day took 12 hours.

The sun was considered to be the most powerful force in Egypt and had several gods associated with it. The main god of the sun was called Re (sometimes written as Ra). Aten and Atum were two other sun-gods.

When different gods represented the same thing (such as the sun), they symbolised different activities. The sun travelling across the sky was Re. The Egyptians thought that Re travelled in his sun-boat, making sure that everything on the land was as it should be. The god Aten was the aspect of the sun that gave life to all living things and was shown as the disk of the sun with its rays ending in hands. Aten made living things grow and flourish. Atum's powers were similar to Aten's.

Throughout Egyptian history the Egyptians had lots of gods. However, for a short time in around 1300 BC, a pharaoh called Akhenaten changed the religion of Egypt. He created a new religion, based on the old, but with only one god. Akhenaten's god, as his name suggests, was Aten.

Right: Akhenaten and his wife Nefertiti pouring oil offerings to Aten whose rays end in hands. Aten is holding the *ankh* (symbol of life) to Akenaten's nose so that he can breathe it in and live forever.

Akhenaten wrote several hymns to his god, like this one:

> *Splendid you rise, O living Aten, eternal lord!*
> *You are radiant, beautiful, strong.*
> *Your love is great, immense.*
> *Your rays light up all faces.*
> *Your bright hue gives life to hearts*
> *When you fill the land with your love.*

However, most Egyptians did not like having only one god to take care of everything, so few of them followed the new religion for long. Some of them continued to pray to the other gods as well as to Aten. As soon as Akhenaten died, the Egyptians went back to their many different gods.

> The scarab (or dung) beetle was a symbol of the sun. This is because scarab beetles can be seen pushing along a ball of dung containing their eggs. From this ball the baby beetles are born. To the Egyptians, the ball of dung represented the sun.

The pharaoh himself was associated with several gods. While he was alive and ruling he was closely identified with the hawk-headed god, Horus. One of the king's titles was Golden Horus. But when the king died he was then identified with Osiris, Horus' father, who ruled over everything in the afterlife.

Osiris was the god of plants. To the Egyptians, plants seemed to grow, die and come back to life each year. The Egyptians believed that they themselves would come back to life after death. Because of this, Osiris was the god of eternal life and therefore of the afterlife. He is always shown in pictures as a mummified man wearing a crown and holding a crook and flail.

Above: The crook and flail, symbols of a ruler. The crook is for looking after people, while the flail (like a whip) is for punishing them.

Right: A statue of Horus as a hawk, wearing the double crown of Upper and Lower Egypt (by the entrance to the temple at Edfu). Which god or goddess, with a horned sun disc, can you see on the wall behind? (*See gallery, page 30.*)

Osiris beds, which are shallow wooden cases in the shape of Osiris, were filled with Nile mud and planted with grain and placed in some Egyptian tombs, like that of Tutankhamun. The plants would grow in the tomb, meaning that the dead person would live forever.

You can make an Osiris bed by cutting some cotton (cotton wool) in the shape of Osiris. Wet the cotton wool and put some cress, wheat or other seeds on it. Cover the seeds with a damp paper towel. Keep your Osiris bed damp and the seeds will sprout in a few days.

The goddess Isis was the sister of Osiris, but was also his wife. She was therefore the mother of Horus. She was also a very wise and powerful magician and is one of the most famous goddesses.

Isis is often shown as a woman with a throne on her head. The throne is her symbol, possibly because her son Horus, the first king of Egypt, sat on her lap. Her lap was thought of as Horus' throne. Isis was worshipped in many places but especially at the temple of Philae in Upper Egypt.

Isis, with the throne on her head

Left: There is still a special temple to Hathor at Denderah. The tops of many of the columns of the temple are in the shape of Hathor's head.

In later Egyptian history, especially after 900 BC when Egypt was occupied by foreigners who did not understand everything about Egyptian religion, Isis was confused with another goddess called Hathor. Hathor was shown as a cow, or a woman with cow's ears, or a woman with a headdress made of cow's horns with the sun disk in between them.

Hathor was the goddess of beauty, love, music, trees and dancing. She was also the goddess of mines, especially turquoise mines. Many writings about her and drawings of her have been found at ancient mines in Egypt. Hathor was especially worshipped at the temple of Denderah in Upper Egypt.

Seth was the brother of Osiris and Isis. He was the god of many things: disorder, deserts, storms and war. He was shown as a man with the head of a strange animal. According to the legends, Seth did not always get on well with his family and often fought with them.

One of the most important gods in the New Kingdom was Amun, whose name means "the hidden one". He was later joined with the god Re to make the god Amun-Re. Amun-Re was the god who knew everything that was secret, as well as everything on earth. He wears a great crown with two ostrich feathers.

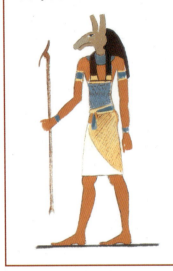

Egyptologists and zoologists are still not sure what animal's head Seth had. What do *you* think it is?

The biggest Egyptian temple of all, at Karnak near Luxor, is dedicated to Amun-Re. His sacred animals were the ram and the duck. Amun's wife was the goddess Mut, who is sometimes shown as a woman wearing a vulture headdress.

Left: The god Amun wearing his double-feathered ostrich crown, giving the *ankh* sign of life to the pharaoh (at Karnak temple).

Above: Ram-headed sphinxes leading to the pylon at Karnak temple. The ram was the symbol of Amun, to whom the temple was dedicated.

The ancient Egyptian word for mother was "mut", and the hieroglyph that represented that word was a vulture. Vultures are supposed to be very good mothers who look after their babies well; they give them their own food and protect them against any attack.

Later, Mut was also shown as a woman with the head of a lioness. Lionesses are also very protective of their young. Mut looks like other goddesses with cats' heads, such as Bastet the cat-goddess, and Sekhmet the warrior-goddess with a lion's head. Today, it is sometimes difficult to tell some similar-looking gods and goddesses from each other, unless their names are written beside them.

Right: The goddess Mut-Sekhmet holding a lotus flower.

Khonsu, the moon-god, was the son of Mut and Amun and was shown as a young boy with a crescent moon on his head.

Above: A big temple to Thoth was built in El-Ashmunein. All that is left is this giant statue of a baboon that stands over three metres tall.

Left: Thoth as an ibis-headed man, wearing a moon disk on his head.

Thoth was the god of writing. He is often associated with two animals: the ibis, which is a bird with a long curved beak, and the baboon. He is often shown as a man with an ibis head and sometimes as a baboon. Because Thoth created writing, he was thought to be very wise and have magical powers, like Isis.

Anubis was the god of cemeteries who took people from this life to the next. He was also the god of mummification, and many tombs contain pictures of him mummifying the dead person. He was shown as a dog or jackal (animals often found in cemeteries) or as a man with the head of one of those animals.

Above: Anubis greeting the dead person. Priests of Anubis often dressed up to look like their god, by wearing a mask.

Sobek was a crocodile god. In his temple at Kom Ombo priests kept pet crocodiles in a large pond. Some of the crocodiles wore gold earrings and even had their nails painted with gold! When the crocodiles died they were mummified and buried in a large tomb. There are still over 300 crocodile mummies at Kom Ombo.

Khnum was a ram-headed god with a human body. He was the creator god. According to one ancient Egyptian story, Khnum made each person out of clay on his potter's wheel and gave them life before putting them in their mother's womb.

Temples

The ancient Egyptians worshipped their gods in temples. The temples were thought to be the house of the god, and were built of stone to last forever because the gods lived forever. People's houses and even the king's palaces were built of mud bricks because people do *not* live forever.

Temples were decorated with pictures showing the lives of the gods and pharaohs, and of the pharaoh making offerings to the gods. Priests kept the temple clean, prayed to the gods and worked in the temple buildings and gardens.

Below. The entrance of a typical temple. An avenue of sphinxes leads up to a pair of obelisks, statues and the pylon. The small picture shows a view of the whole temple.

Inside the temple stood the main statue of the god, often made of gold. Egyptologists think that the Egyptians believed the spirit of the god entered the statue when anyone prayed to it. The priests used to wash the statue, dress it and put food in front of it as offerings to the god.

Sometimes the statue of the god would be taken out onto the temple lake in a boat so that the god could enjoy the fresh air and see his home. It would also be taken up to the roof of the temple by the priests for special prayers and rituals for the rising and setting of the sun.

Not everyone was allowed to see the statue of the god. Only the priests and the pharaoh, who was considered a god himself, went into the god's rooms. Other people would pray to the god outside, or in the courtyard of the temple.

People would see the god only when the statue was taken out on parade at a festival. Sometimes they carved their prayers on a piece of stone called a "stela", or made statues of themselves that they left in the temple for the gods.

Left: Two bald-headed Sem (or funeral) priests from the tomb of Userhet in Thebes. Their uniform includes a leopard skin. One is pouring an offering and the other is burning incense.
Above left: A statue of a man holding a stela. The man's prayers to the god are written on the stela. When the statue was given to a god and stood in a temple, it was as if his prayers were always being said in the temple.
Above right: A granite stela from a temple, showing a king making an offering to the god Re-Harakhte.

People approached a temple from a long avenue that was lined with sphinxes. Sphinxes usually have the body of a lion and the head of a pharaoh, and are a symbol of the pharaoh.

The avenue led to the temple gate, called a pylon. The pylon was made of two huge walls with a gate in the middle. Statues of pharaohs and obelisks, which are tall blocks of stone with small pyramids on top, stood in front of the pylon. Flags flew from the pylon. Inside the pylon was a staircase that led to the top. From the top of the pylon trumpeters blew their trumpets before the start of a festival, or when the pharaoh wanted to make an announcement.

The pylon was decorated with scenes of the pharaoh defeating his enemies and looking after the safety of Egypt with the help of the gods. This part of the temple was the part most often seen by people, as the rest of the temple was surrounded by a huge brick wall.

Behind the pylon was an open court with pillars along the sides where sometimes people were allowed to enter and pray, or to leave their written prayers. After this court was another room called a hypostyle hall, which means that its roof was supported by lots of columns. The tops of the columns were carved in the shape of lotus and papyrus plants, as well as other plants like palm trees.

Left: The pylon of the temple at Luxor, with an obelisk and statues of Ramesses II. There were originally two obelisks (the other is now in Paris). The pylon walls are covered with carvings that describe Ramesses II's victory in a great battle.

Right: The tops of columns are called capitals, and were based on Egyptian plants

Behind this hall was the inner sanctuary where the statue of the god was kept. The statue might have been made of stone and gold, or just of gold, decorated with jewellery. It was probably not more than 50 centimetres (20 inches) tall. No statues of gods from temple sanctuaries have ever been found, so we are not sure of what they were made or what size they really were.

Around the sanctuary were several rooms for storing the gold, perfumes, jewellery, cloth, make-up, golden and silver bowls, and furniture for the god. Sometimes there was a court behind the sanctuary with more statues.

The group of rooms, halls and courtyards was surrounded by a long wall. Temple walls were always decorated with pictures of the pharaohs and the gods, as well as hieroglyphs telling stories of the gods or listing the offerings that the kings had given to them.

Below: The pharaoh Hatshepsut offering sacred oils to Amun. who has two ostrich feathers on his head.

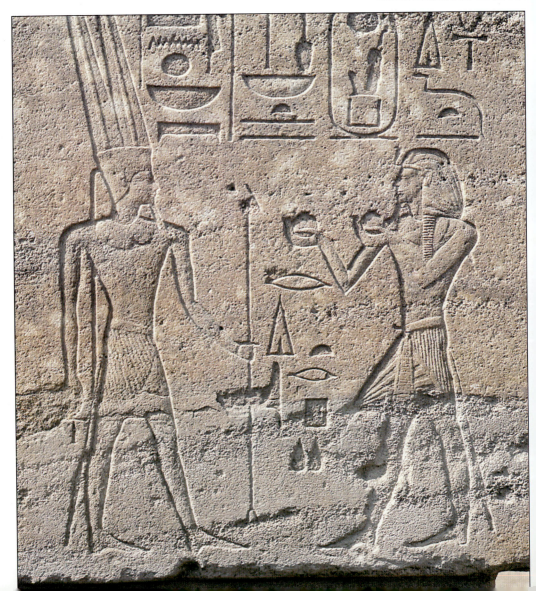

The temple did not consist of one building only. Inside the temple wall there were also other buildings and often large areas of land for vegetables and animals. There were granaries, libraries, hospitals, schools, gardens, small farms, lakes, wells, kitchens, and workshops which made tools, furniture, dishes, chariots, jewellery and perfumes.

Below. Priests gardening and farming in the temple beside the holy lake.

All the people who worked for the pharaoh were paid from the treasuries and granaries that stood inside the temples themselves. If there was ever any danger of attack by desert tribes, people hid inside the temples, which were easy to defend because of their high stone walls. The thick mud-brick walls surrounding the temple, its buildings and land, also helped to defend it from attack.

Priests

Most priests lived and worked in the temple all year. Other, usually poorer people, who worked in temples for three or four months of the year while they were not farming. They did not have important positions, but the temple provided them with food and clothes as part of their payment.

Many different priests, including women, worked in the temple. The most important was the High Priest, who was the chief priest of the temple after the pharaoh. The most important priestess was the "god's wife", or High Priestess. All other priests and priestesses served under these two.

Some priestesses and priests worked as temple dancers and musicians, while others prayed to the gods all the time or performed different tasks in the temple and its workshops. Whenever the god was taken out for a parade or to visit another temple, the priests and priestesses went with the statue. Some carried the shrine or box in which the statue stood. Others walked in front, dancing, playing music and chanting.

Most priests and priestesses wore plain white linen and had either bare feet or wore sandals. Some of them also wore leopard skins over their clothes. Many priests had their heads shaved, so it is easy to recognise them in temple and tomb paintings.

Worship

Generally, people worshipped gods at home, or at smaller shrines, and not in the temple. They often had shrines to their favourite gods in their houses. A house-shrine contained a statue of the god, and a place to put incense, flowers and offerings to the god.

Different professions worshipped different gods. Scribes kept statues of Thoth, musicians had statues of Hathor, and embalmers had statues of Anubis. There were two special gods who were the protectors of families and pregnant women: the dwarf-lion-god Bes and Tawasret, the hippopotamus-lion-goddess. Paintings of these gods are often found in ancient Egyptian houses.

Right: Bes, with a dwarf's body and lion's head, guarding the temple at Denderah.

Make your own amulet out of paper, clay or dough and wear it for good luck!

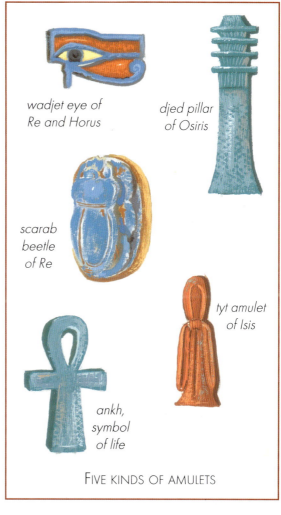

wadjet eye of Re and Horus

djed pillar of Osiris

scarab beetle of Re

tyt amulet of Isis

ankh, symbol of life

FIVE KINDS OF AMULETS

People often hung amulets in the shape of their favourite gods, or in the shape of the gods' symbols, around their necks. The favourite Egyptian amulet was the *wadjet* (eye of Horus) that protected people from evil spirits. Another favourite was the *ankh* – or key of life – that gave the wearer a long life. The scarab beetle and figures of Bes were also popular amulets.

All these amulets were supposed to protect the wearer from evil, or to help bring good luck. Amulets were also placed on bodies that were going to be mummified and buried.

Festivals

Festivals were an important part of ancient Egyptian religion. Some festivals were celebrated when the statue of the god went to visit his wife in another temple, or when he "marched" around the town every year to protect it. People from everywhere would come to join the celebration, a special market supplied food and drink, while entertainers such as acrobats and actors performed for the crowds. Even the priests of the temple dressed up as gods and performed plays about the lives of the gods.

A big procession with the temple musicians, singers, dancers, priests and the god's statue paraded through the town. The statue was placed into a shrine that was put in a model boat and carried on the shoulders of the priests. People were able to see the god and pray to him. They could ask him "yes/no" questions about their lives. If the god's answer was "yes", then the god would magically force the model boat to move forward. If it was "no", the boat moved backward.

The ancient Egyptian religion was practised for thousands of years, even when the Romans ruled the country. In the 4th century AD Egypt, like the rest of the Roman Empire, became Christian. Today, following the introduction of Islam in the 7th century, most Egyptians are Muslims.

Gallery of gods

This shows just a few of the important Egyptian gods, who numbered several hundred altogether

Amun-Re
a chief god

Anubis
god of mummification

Bastet
goddess of war

Bes
god of protection and childbirth

Hathor
goddess of love

Horus
god of the pharaoh

Isis
goddess of magic

Khnum
god of floods

Khonsu
god of the new moon

Mut
goddess of motherhood

Osiris
god of the afterlife

Ptah
god of creativity

Re
sun god

Sekhmet
goddess of destruction

Seth
god of disorder

Sobek
god of the Fayoum

Tawasret
goddess of childbirth

Thoth
god of writing and learning

Glossary

afterlife — life after death

amulet — a piece of jewellery worn as protection against evil

pylon — a large gateway at the entrance to a temple

sanctuary — the holiest part of a temple, where the main altar and statue of the god were found

shrine — a small place or box for worshipping a god, at home, by the side of a road, or in a temple

stela — *(plural: stelae)* a large standing stone, decorated with pictures, writing or both

Index

afterlife	3, 5, 8	Hathor	11, 26
Akhenaten	7-8	Hatshepsut	13, 22
amulet	27	hawk	8-9
Amun	12, 14, 21-22	hieroglyphs	13, 22
ankh	7, 12, 27	High Priest	24
Anubis	15, 26	High Priestess	24
Aswan	4	hippopotamus	26
Aten	6-8	Horus	3, 8-10, 27
Atum	6	hymns	7
		hypostyle hall	21
Bastet	13		
Bes	26-27	ibis	14
Book of the Dead	2-3	Isis	10-12
creation	2, 15	jewellery	21-23
crocodile	15		
		Karnak	12-13, 21
dancers	25, 29	Khnum	15
Denderah	10, 26	Khonsu	5, 14
dwarf	26	Kom Ombo	15
Edfu	3, 9	lake	18
El-Ashmunein	14	lion, lioness	20, 26
embalmers	26	lotus	13, 21
festival	20, 28-29	Mereruka	18
		mines	11
Geb	5	moon	5, 14
gold	15, 18, 21-22	mud bricks	16
		mummy	8, 15, 27
Hapi	4	musicians	25, 29

31

Mut	*12-14*	Sem priest	*18*
Nile	*4, 10*	Seth	*12*
Nut	*5*	shrine	*25-26, 29*
		Sobek	*15*
obelisk	*20*	sphinx	*13, 20-21*
Osiris	*8, 10-12*	stela	*19*
		sun	*4, 6, 8, 11*
palm	*21*		
papyrus	*21*	Tawasret	*26*
Philae	*10*	temple	*2-4, 9-26*
priests	*15, 17-19, 24-25, 28-29*	Thoth	*14, 26*
pylon	*20-21*	tomb	*2-3, 5, 16*
pyramid	*20*	Tutankhamun	*10*
Re (Ra)	*6, 12*	vulture	*12-13*
scarab	*8, 27*		
scribes	*26*	*wadjet*	*27*
Sekhmet	*13*	writing	*2, 11, 14*

Photo credits

copyright and photography by Salima Ikram: p3 (from temple of Horus, Edfu); p7 (from Egyptian Museum, Cairo); p9 (from Edfu temple); p12 (from Karnak temple); p13, bottom (from Karnak temple); p14, left (from Valley of the Queens, Thebes); p14, right (from El-Ashmunein temple); p15 (from Valley of the Queens); p19, right (from Egyptian Museum); p22 (from Karnak); p26 (from Denderah)

copyright Hoopoe Books, photography by Ayman El Kharrat:
p2 (from Egyptian Museum); p19, left (from Egyptian Museum)

copyright Hoopoe Books, photography by Tim Loveless:
p13, top (from Karnak temple); p20 (from Luxor temple)

copyright Theban Mapping Project:
p18 (from tomb of Userhet, Thebes)
p11 (from temple of Hathor, Denderah, *photo by Francis Dzikowski*)